MARINE FORCE RECON

U.S. SPECIAL FORCES

MARINE FORCE RECON

JIM WHITING

CREATIVE EDUCATION • CREATIVE PAPERBACKS

PUBLISHED BY Creative Education and Creative Paperbacks
P.O. Box 227, Mankato, Minnesota 56002
Creative Education and Creative Paperbacks are imprints of The Creative Company
www.thecreativecompany.us

DESIGN BY Christine Vanderbeek; **PRODUCTION BY** Liddy Walseth
ART DIRECTION BY Rita Marshall
PRINTED IN CHINA

PHOTOGRAPHS BY
Alamy (AF archive, akg-images, dpa picture alliance archive, Everett Collection, Inc., Moviestore collection Ltd, PJF Military Collection, Trinity Mirror/Mirrorpix, US Marines Photo), DVIDS (SSgt Tyler J. Bolken, Cpl Jonathan Boynes, LCpl Ashley McLaughlin, Cpl Joshua Murray, Sgt Danielle Rodrigues), iStockphoto (spxChrome), Shutterstock (ALMAGAMI, gst)

LIBRARY OF CONGRESS CATALOGING-IN-PUBLICATION DATA
Names: Whiting, Jim, author.
Title: Marine Force Recon / Jim Whiting.
Series: U.S. Special Forces.
Includes bibliographical references and index.
Summary: A chronological account of the American military special forces unit known as Marine Force Recon, including key details about important figures, landmark missions, and controversies.
Identifiers: LCCN 2017027666 / ISBN 978-1-60818-984-7 (hardcover) / ISBN 978-1-62832-611-6 (pbk) / ISBN 978-1-64000-085-8 (eBook)
Subjects: LCSH: 1. United States. Marine Corps. Force Reconnaissance—Juvenile literature. 2. United States. Marine Corps—Commando troops—Juvenile literature. 3. Special forces (Military science)—United States—Juvenile literature.
Classification: LCC VE23.W45 2018 / DDC 359.9/64130973—dc23

CCSS: RI.5.1, 2, 3, 8; RH.6-8.4, 5, 6, 8

FIRST EDITION HC 9 8 7 6 5 4 3 2 1
FIRST EDITION PBK 9 8 7 6 5 4 3 2 1

U.S. SPECIAL FORCES

TABLE OF CONTENTS

The M3 Carl Gustaf is used by forces worldwide and sometimes adds a post-firing booster.

FORCE FACTS The heaviest weapon in the Force Recon arsenal is the 84 mm M3 *recoilless* rifle, nicknamed the "Carl Gustaf" in honor of the Swedish company that manufactures it.

FORCE FACTS After its capture, Tinian became an important U.S. airbase. The planes that dropped atomic bombs on Japan during World War II were based there.

INTRODUCTION

In July 1944, the Second and Fourth Marine Divisions were about to invade the Japanese-held island of Tinian in the western Pacific Ocean. The divisions had just suffered heavy ***casualties*** on nearby Saipan. Planners wanted to minimize further losses. They knew the landing site would be crucial. Some favored two narrow beaches on the island's northwestern coast, code-named White Beach 1 and 2. Others favored Yellow Beach in the southwest. It was wider and more accessible, but most of the island's 9,000 defenders were concentrated there.

The Marine Corps ***Amphibious*** Reconnaissance Battalion evaluated both locations. Armed only with knives, the men paddled ashore in rubber boats one night. They carried out their observations within earshot of Japanese troops. The men assigned to Yellow Beach found it heavily fortified with many obstacles. At White Beach, the natural features were easily surmountable, and there were no significant Japanese obstructions. The decision was made: White Beach would be the site.

To fool the Japanese, a convoy headed toward Yellow Beach. The landing craft got within 400 yards of the beach before turning around. A concealed Japanese battery badly damaged two of the warships. It inflicted more than 300 casualties. But the **feint** kept most of the defenders from opposing the real landing. The Marines coming ashore at White Beach lost fewer men than the ships at Yellow Beach. They quickly took the island. "Had the division gone ashore on [Yellow Beach], it would have been a slaughter," said Lieutenant Russell Corey, who was part of the landing force. "The [Japanese] had gun emplacements and artillery all lined up."

Troops landing at White Beach had to leave their boats and wade around the reefs to get to shore.

KNOWLEDGE IS PRICELESS

U.S. SPECIAL FORCES

THE TINIAN INVASION OFFERS A PRIME EXAMPLE OF THE importance of knowing the positions and strength of an enemy. The secret gathering of this knowledge is known as reconnaissance, or recon, and history is packed with examples of the consequences of ignoring it. One of the most famous instances occurred in A.D. 9. A Roman general named Varus led three heavily armed legions through the Teutoburg Forest in Germany. Varus hadn't done any recon. He had no idea that thousands of fierce German warriors were lurking nearby. Nearly all 15,000 of his troops were slaughtered. Many historians consider this battle to be Rome's greatest military defeat.

When World War I ended in 1918, Japan was granted control over many remote islands in the central Pacific Ocean. A Marine officer, Major Earl H. "Pete" Ellis, predicted the likelihood that Japan would initiate a war with the United States. He recognized the strategic importance of those islands in such a conflict. He traveled there "for the purposes of conducting the necessary reconnaissance." He wrote a 30,000-word report about his observations in 1921. It later became the basis for War Plan Orange. This plan laid out the basic elements of the U.S. strategy in the Pacific more than 20 years later in World War II. However, in the meantime, the Marine Corps made little effort at follow-up reconnaissance of what would eventually be their primary battlegrounds.

The attack on Pearl Harbor on December 7, 1941, spurred action. Early in 1942, an "Observer Group" of 2 officers and 20

Hot-air balloons were used during World War I to gain a bird's-eye view of the front line.

FORCE FACTS Zodiac rubber rafts are typically more than 15 feet (4.6 m) in length and can attain speeds in excess of 20 miles (32 km) an hour.

enlisted men became the first formal Marine unit trained to conduct amphibious recon. A year later, the group increased to 6 officers and 92 enlisted men. It was renamed the Amphibious Reconnaissance Company (ARC). The company went ashore on the *atolls* of Apamama, Majuro, and Eniwetok and gathered valuable information for the larger units that would soon attack. The ARC added personnel as the Marines began assaulting the islands that Ellis had been concerned about. By April 1944, the group boasted 20 officers, 270 enlisted men, and 13 navy medical personnel. It was now called the Amphibious Reconnaissance Battalion. It proved its worth at Tinian and conducted more than 100 other missions.

The battalion was reduced in size but continued training when the war ended in 1945. It returned to action during the Korean War (1950–53) and carried out numerous missions. Some were in conjunction with the navy's Underwater Demolition Teams (UDTs, today known as SEALs) in coastal areas. Others involved penetrating as deep as 40 miles (65 km) into enemy territory. After that conflict, it became clear that Marines would not be limited to amphibious operations. Future battlefields would cover many more square miles than the Pacific islands. Now known as Marine Force Recon, the group began training for *insertions* using helicopters and parachutes. Recon Marines became the first American servicemen to develop free-fall parachute techniques.

The value of Force Recon was further proven during the Vietnam War (1955–75). Force Recon members began arriving in Vietnam in 1965. Almost all their missions involved helicopter insertions and lasted for five or six days. The amphibious operations that had characterized the group's purpose in World War II were largely conducted by the newly formed SEALs. Force Recon troops learned new techniques, exemplified by the terms "Key Hole" and "Sting Ray." Key Hole missions emphasized secrecy

Force Recon embarks on missions using various methods, including parachutes, helicopters, and boats.

FORCE FACTS At the height of the Vietnam War, as many as 40 Force Recon teams were in action at once.

and stealth. Their purpose was to discover information about the enemy, such as the number and locations of troops, campsites, and weaponry, without letting the enemy know they were there. Troops patrolled in small teams, usually consisting of four men. They carried light weapons. These were used only to help them escape if they were discovered. To avoid detection, the men often used a "bait-and-switch" technique. They would set up camp at dusk and then move elsewhere soon afterward. "On a number of occasions," a Force Recon officer said, "teams moved and then reported seeing NVA [North Vietnamese Army] sweeping the area they left." Sting Ray missions, on the other hand, took place relatively close to American lines. These men were heavily armed. They deliberately sought contact with opposing forces, often so they could call in artillery strikes. These missions helped compile a remarkable statistic: Force Recon Marines had a kill rate of 34 enemy soldiers for every 1 of their own. The ratio among regular Marines was less than 8 to 1.

Recon Marines are trained to maneuver inflatable Zodiac boats in all types of conditions.

When the war ended, Force Recon was deactivated. It was reactivated in 1986 and deployed four years later during the first Gulf War. This was its introduction to the Middle East, where many of its missions have taken place since. Force Recon played a key role in Operation Iraqi Freedom, participating in both the 2003 invasion of Iraq and the subsequent occupation of the country.

A major change came three years after the Iraqi invasion. In the mid-1980s, the U.S. Special Operations Command (SOCOM) had been established to combat the rising threat of terrorism. A separate unit within the U.S. military, SOCOM had its own command structure. The navy, army, and air

force, whose special operations forces (SOFs) were now controlled by SOCOM, all contributed personnel. The Marine Corps didn't join SOCOM, in large part because it didn't want to lose control of its elite units, such as Force Recon. But after the terrorist attacks on September 11, 2001, the number of Special Forces missions increased dramatically. SOCOM needed more active-duty soldiers on the ground. So the newly established Marine Special Operations Command (MARSOC) became operational in 2006. Most of its members came from Force Recon. The remaining Force Recon personnel were assigned to various Marine divisions.

Top Marine officers soon realized that the corps still needed the skills Force Recon had provided. It was reestablished two years later, with three companies. Each company

When performing recon missions, troops evaluate the numbers, strengths, and behaviors of the enemy.

is attached to a Marine Expeditionary Force (MEF), which is the principal war-fighting unit of the Marine Corps. An MEF consists of a full division, an aircraft wing, a logistics group, and several smaller units. It is self-sustaining in combat for at least 60 days. Today, MARSOC takes on the role of direct action (like the Vietnam-era Sting Ray missions). Force Recon focuses primarily on ***intelligence*** gathering. It also participates in the specialized area of Visit, Board, Search, and Seizure (VBSS). In VBSS, Force Recon platoons provide the assault element in seizing enemy vessels and combating piracy.

A Force Recon company consists of several groups. One is company headquarters, composed of the commanding and executive officers and a sergeant major. Five other elements—administrative, intelligence, operations, logistics and supply, and communications—provide vital support. At the heart of the company are five or six Force Recon platoons. Each platoon consists of the commander, platoon sergeant, radio operator, navy medic, equipment noncommissioned officer (NCO), and three or four six-man reconnaissance teams.

During their missions in the field, the recon team is headed by the point man. This person carries the lightest pack because he is responsible for leading the team in the right direction. He is continuously on the lookout for ***improvised*** explosive devices (IEDs). Next in line is the team leader, followed by the radio operator, and then the assistant radio operator. Fifth is the "slack man." This is usually the team's newest member. He's likely to pack the heaviest load, which may include a machine gun for extra firepower. The assistant team leader brings up the rear and makes sure no one is left behind.

★★★

Marine Force Recon trainees learn navigation skills on land and in water.

FORCE FACTS When fast-roping or rappelling, soldiers wear heavy gloves to keep their hands from shredding on the rope.

JOINING FORCE RECON

U.S. SPECIAL FORCES

UNSURPRISINGLY, BECOMING A MEMBER OF THE ELITE FORCE RECON is difficult. First, candidates must score at least a mark of 105 on the Armed Services Vocational Aptitude Battery (ASVAB) test. They must also pass a stringent physical fitness test that includes sit-ups, pull-ups, and a three-mile (4.8 km) run. A perfect score of 300 is achieved by completing 100 sit-ups in 2 minutes, 20 pull-ups with a full stop between each, and the run in 18 minutes. To pass, candidates need to score at least 225. Potential Force Recon Marines must also be eligible for a security clearance, have a stellar service record, and have at least 18 months remaining in their term of service. In addition, they must achieve an expert marksmanship rating during basic training.

The next step is the rigorous 48-hour recon screening. This includes swimming 550 yards (500 m) in 13 minutes, a 27-yard (25 m) underwater swim, and a deep-water rifle retrieval followed by a 55-yard (50 m) swim with the weapon held overhead. (A concrete block may substitute for a weapon in the retrieval and accompanying swim.) Other water tests require the trainee to jump into water from a height of 25 feet (7.6 m) while wearing combat gear and then tread water for half an hour. A battery of physical tests follows immediately. Then candidates do multiple repetitions of an obstacle course. The amount of effort a candidate puts forth is more important than the time it takes to complete the course. The Marines also complete a lengthy, fast-paced hike with a 50-pound (23 kg) sandbag in their *rucksacks*. Those who can't keep up are dropped from consideration. The

Hiking with 50-pound (23 kg) packs—and carrying additional containers full of sand—is all in a day's training.

FORCE FACTS Camp Pendleton was established in 1942 to train Marines for combat in the Pacific. It is named after Major General Joseph H. Pendleton, a longtime advocate for West Coast Marine training.

process concludes with a lengthy interview to evaluate the candidate's suitability to continue.

Many Marines fail the first time. They are allowed to take the screening as often as they want. Multiple attempts speak highly of their motivation. Money isn't part of that motivation. With few exceptions, Force Recon members are paid the same as other Marines of equal rank and length of service.

Those who pass recon screening take the 59-day Basic Reconnaissance Course (BRC). This three-phase course is held at California's Camp Pendleton, situated between Los Angeles and San Diego. Phase 1 focuses on cultivating physical skills. Trainees do a lot of running and high-repetition physical training to develop stamina. They also negotiate obstacle courses, learn land navigation with a map and compass, do numerous fast hikes wearing a rucksack over steadily increasing distances with steadily increasing weights, and swim in the ocean. The ocean temperatures vary widely, from a relatively balmy 75 to 80 °F (24 to 27 °C) in July and August to a bone-chilling 45 to 59 °F (7 to 15 °C) in February.

Some of the most important skills trainees practice are helicopter rope suspension techniques (HRST). HRST are used in insertions and ***extractions*** where helicopters cannot land. These methods include fast-roping, in which the Marine uses his hands and feet to slide down a thick rope as quickly as possible. Because several men can be on the same rope, this is the fastest method of insertion. Another is rappelling, in which the Marine coils a rope secured to the helicopter around his body and slides down. Only one man can be on the rope at a time.

A third is Jacob's ladder, a flexible ladder especially useful for extractions. Perhaps the most dramatic is Special Personnel Insertion/Extraction (SPIE), in which several men wearing harnesses hook themselves onto D-rings that are fastened to a rope suspended from a helicopter. The aircraft lifts off with the men dangling beneath it and carries them to a secure insert zone.

Fast-roping and other HRST are practiced from land-based towers as well as aircraft.

FORCE FACTS The combatant diver course includes learning how to use a rebreather, which recirculates the breathing gas a diver uses to avoid the telltale stream of bubbles from conventional scuba gear.

Force Recon developed this technique during the Vietnam War.

Another method of debarkation from a chopper is helocasting. This procedure requires a Marine to jump from the helicopter into the water and swim to shore.

Force Recon Marines also use parachutes when their objective is beyond helicopter range and absolute quiet and stealth are required. The men exit the aircraft at heights of up to seven miles (11.3 km) and glide silently toward the ground. Special harnesses enable them to carry a fully loaded rucksack or other equipment. Some of these insertions are classified as high altitude–high opening (HAHO). The jumper opens his chute—often a ***parafoil***—within moments of exiting the aircraft. He uses a ***Global Positioning System*** (GPS) or other navigational tool to head toward the target, which can be up to 40 miles (64.4 km) away. In high altitude–low opening (HALO) operations, the Marine free-falls most of the distance to the ground before deploying the chute.

Phase 2 of the BRC lasts three weeks. It concentrates on the tactics for successful small-unit operations, culminating in a nine-day exercise under conditions the men are likely to encounter in the real world. The final two weeks of training, Phase 3, shifts southward to Coronado, across the bay from San Diego. There the trainees learn to navigate on the open ocean. One of the challenges is to land a Zodiac rubber boat in breakers several feet high, and then launch the craft back into the surf when a mission is complete.

Recon soldiers must be able to carry their gear, weighing 50 pounds (22.7 kg) or more, through the water.

After finishing the course, newly minted Force Recon operators are assigned to the Force Recon companies attached to one of the three MEFs. Their training is far from over. There are many advanced courses the men can take to become even more proficient. Some, such as those to become a combatant

diver or a scout sniper, are offered by the Marine Corps. Others involve different branches of the military. For example, the army conducts a three-week Airborne School as well as Ranger School, which GoArmy.com terms "the most physically and mentally demanding leadership school the army has to offer."

Helocasting requires soldiers to jump out of a helicopter into the water and swim to shore while fully clothed.

In the field, Force Recon missions are divided into green operations and black operations. These are similar to the Vietnam-era Key Hole and Sting Ray classifications. Green operations involve a mixture of amphibious and ground reconnaissance. There is no intentional enemy contact. Relying on their stealth, the men go inland for many miles, well beyond the reach of artillery support. Many missions are conducted in advance of an attack by a Marine unit. Sometimes, Force Recon troops take soil samples of a proposed landing site. Other times, they examine inland terrain with special emphasis on roads, bridges, and other ***infrastructure***. They also place remote sensors to guide incoming troops and identify possible areas for helicopter landings and airborne drop zones. Some missions occur during or after an incursion, such as battle damage assessment. In most cases, a green operation is judged a failure if even a single shot is fired.

On the other hand, black operations are likely to involve gunfire. They incorporate direct action against an enemy and often take place within range of artillery or nearby air support. With MARSOC taking on many of the black operations that Force Recon previously would have done, Force Recon has become somewhat specialized. Some examples of black operations include seizing oil platforms, calling in air strikes, and conducting VBSS missions.

To carry out their operations, Force Recon troops use many of the same weapons as other Special Forces. The basic weapon is the M4A1 carbine. It accommodates a host of accessories. A *foregrip* increases control over the gun. A sound suppressor cuts down on noise. A side-mounted rail allows for the attachment of several types of sights for both night and day use. One is the reflex, or red dot, sight. This "paints" a target with a red dot. The M203 grenade launcher can be attached under an M4A1's barrel. It fires a variety of grenades—*fragmentation*, concussion, and *incendiary*—though many operators prefer a stun or flash-bang grenade. These momentarily distract and disorient the enemy. Often, that is all the time the Marines need to gain the upper hand.

Other firearms include shotguns for *breaching* doors and several sniper and marksman rifles. Force Recon personnel can choose from a variety of handguns. The recently introduced Colt M45A1 pistol, with its distinctive desert-tan color, has become increasingly popular. For more firepower, the men call upon the reliable M249 *squad automatic weapon*. Recently, however, the M27 infantry automatic rifle has been replacing the M249 because it is lighter and easier to carry.

A green operation requires stealth and is considered a failure if just a single shot was fired.

FORCE FACTS Sample ASVAB questions are: 1) If there are three quarts of gas in a gallon container, how full is the container? A. 50% B. 60% C. 75% D. 80%; 2) *Observe* most nearly means: A. maintain B. watch C. organize D. protest

VENGEANCE HAS A NAME
WAR ZONE
PUNISHER
IN THEATERS DECEMBER 5
[NYSE LGF]
LIONSGATE
MARVEL

FORCE RECON IN FICTION—AND IN FACT

U.S. SPECIAL FORCES

Even though relatively few people outside the military are familiar with Force Recon, it has a surprisingly large number of media portrayals. Perhaps the first was the fictional Frank Castle, who originally appeared in a Spiderman comic book in 1974. A former member of Force Recon, Castle also trained with other special operations forces and has a variety of combat skills. When a mob boss murders Castle's family, he becomes Punisher, a vigilante who seeks revenge.

Since then, Punisher has been the hero in dozens of other comic-book series. He takes on almost every criminal organization in the world, usually doing so in especially gruesome fashion. The Punisher also appears in other genres. These include five graphic novels in the late 1980s and early 1990s. Six Nintendo video games made between 1990 and 2009 also feature the character. The 1989 movie *The Punisher* stars Dolph Lundgren as Castle. A 2004 remake casts Thomas Jane as Castle and John Travolta as his primary antagonist. The character even had an effect on real-life special forces. Navy SEAL sniper Chris Kyle said his platoon adopted Punisher's skull symbol as its emblem. "What the Punisher did was cool," Kyle added. "He righted wrongs. He killed bad guys."

The leading characters of a number of other action films are also former Force Recon personnel who put their military training to good use. These include Chance Boudreaux, played by Jean-Claude Van Damme, in *Hard Target* (1993). He helps a woman searching for her father, a homeless veteran who is the object of a deadly game of hide-and-seek, targeted by a wealthy man. In *U.S. Marshals*

Punisher: War Zone, *released in 2008, was the third reboot of the fictional Frank Castle on the big screen.*

FORCE FACTS Evan Wright's book, *Generation Kill*, won the 2005 General Wallace M. Greene Jr. award from the Marine Corps Heritage Foundation for the best nonfiction account of Marines and Marine Corps life.

(1998), Mark Sheridan (Wesley Snipes) tries to clear himself of the murder charges that are pinned on him after an operation to find a ***mole*** in the U.S. State Department goes off the rails. Val Kilmer plays Robert Scott in *Spartan* (2004). He heads up a team searching for the president's kidnapped daughter. Denzel Washington's character, John Creasy, in *Man on Fire* (2004) goes on a rampage after the little girl he was hired to protect in Mexico City is kidnapped. In *Shooter* (2007), Mark Wahlberg's character, a Force Recon sniper named Bob Lee Swagger, is framed for murder. Jake Sully (played by Sam Worthington) is a one-time Force Recon Marine who stars in the science-fiction film *Avatar* (2009). He is a paraplegic who hopes to regain use of his legs.

Perhaps the best-known movie showing Force Recon in action is *Heartbreak Ridge* (1986). Clint Eastwood stars as Marine Gunnery Sergeant Tom Highway, who was awarded the Medal of Honor for his actions at Heartbreak Ridge during the Korean War. On the verge of retirement, Highway takes command of an undisciplined and undertrained reconnaissance platoon. He works them hard to make them a better unit. He then leads them in the 1983 invasion of the Caribbean island of Grenada. His training helps the platoon succeed in their mission. The Marine Corps initially supported the film and even let the producers use Camp Pendleton for some scenes. For a variety of reasons, they later withdrew that support. Individual Marines also criticized *Heartbreak Ridge*, saying it misrepresented them and that many of Highway's training methods were inaccurate.

In *Sniper* (1993), Tom Berenger and Billy Zane play Force Recon snipers. Their mission is to kill a Colombian general allied with a drug kingpin. The film generated six straight-to-video sequels. The most recent, *Sniper: Homeland Security*, was released in 2017.

The Rock (1996) takes a vastly different perspective on Force Recon. Former Brigadier General Frank Hummel (Ed Harris) is furious with the government for not compensating the families of

Hollywood has based many films around recon missions, both factual and fictional.

Marines who died on secret missions while under his command. The general and a group of rogue Force Recon troops seize control of the former prison on Alcatraz Island in San Francisco Bay. They take nearly 100 tourists hostage and threaten to launch missiles filled with deadly gas unless the government pays $100 million to the families of the fallen troops. While no one could take the film seriously as a portrayal of actual Force Recon Marines, many critics liked it. "*The Rock* is a first-rate, slam-bang action thriller with a lot of style and no little humor," said Roger Ebert of the *Chicago Tribune*. *The Rock* might also have generated a bit of inter-service rivalry. At one point, Hummel and his former Marines easily dispose of a Navy SEAL team that tries to capture them.

Several video games include Force Recon characters. For example, the 2011 game *Crysis 2* features Alcatraz, a Force Recon Marine who wears the Nanosuit 2.0 as he battles to save New York City from aliens. *Official Xbox Magazine* gave it a 9/10 rating. A novel by Canadian science-fiction author Peter Watts, *Crysis: Legion*, is a tie-in to the game. Former Force Recon Captain Alex Mason headlines 2010's *Call of Duty: Black Ops*. Within its first 24 hours, the game sold nearly 6 million copies. It has two sequels: *Call of Duty: Black Ops II* (2012) and *Call of Duty: Black Ops III* (2015). In *Call of Duty 4: Modern Warfare*, Force Recon Sergeant Paul Jackson fights terrorism in the Middle East and a civil war in Russia. It was the best-selling game worldwide in 2007.

In The Rock, *Nicolas Cage (below) tries to stop a group of rogue Force Recon Marines from launching nerve gas from Alcatraz.*

Generation Kill, a 2008 HBO miniseries, was nominated for 11 Primetime Emmy Awards. The show was based on the book by **embedded** journalist Evan Wright. It follows Second Platoon, Bravo Company of the First Reconnaissance Battalion during the 2003 invasion of Iraq. Most critics liked the series. So did several hundred Marines who attended a special screening at Camp Pendleton before the official showing. "The episodes

FORCE FACTS The USA television network premiered *Shooter*, based on the 2007 movie starring Mark Wahlberg, in November 2016. Ryan Philippe plays Bob Lee Swagger.

got high marks for realism, right down to details like the pizzas that were delivered from Kuwait as Marines waited for the invasion to begin," said Tony Perry of the *Los Angeles Times*. It wasn't all fun and games, though. The audience fell silent when firefights erupted onscreen. "This is the real story about the real guys," said technical adviser and former Staff Sergeant Eric Kocher, who took part in the invasion.

The "real guys" depicted in the series felt the same way as the Camp Pendleton audience. "At the end of the day, it was real events," said one. "No matter how gritty or politically incorrect, it was real life." Another said that it gave him the chance to share his wartime experiences with his wife, which brought them closer together. He estimated that the events portrayed were about 60 to 70 percent accurate, though the discrepancies were relatively minor. A third said, "I've spoken to sailors and soldiers and Marines and airmen. Almost to the man or woman, the *Generation Kill* book and following show seemed to resonate so strongly. It didn't matter that it was a Marine unit that was being portrayed."

Several book series feature Force Recon as well. Between 1999 and 2003, author James V. Smith wrote the six-book Force Recon series. Captain Jack Swayne heads up a four-man group called Team Midnight. The team tackles a number of highly dangerous missions, often without official support. The subtitle of the first book—"Search, Destroy, Survive"—is the theme of the entire series. In 1998, Matthew Reilly's book *Ice Station* introduced readers to Captain Shane "Scarecrow" Schofield. He leads Force Recon teams through a number of adventures that many readers describe as unrealistic yet great fun to read. The fifth book in the series, *Scarecrow Returns*, was published in 2012. Abigail Roux's nine-book series Cut & Run, which began in 2008, features FBI special agent Ty Grady, a former Force Recon staff sergeant. Roux's four-book Sidewinder series is a spinoff of Cut & Run. It focuses on several members of Grady's old Force Recon team.

Generation Kill *was inspired by Master Sergeant Brad Colbert, who speaks to fellow service members about choosing healthier lifestyles.*

FORCE FACTS Several episodes of *Generation Kill* include an actor portraying Marine General James "Mad Dog" Mattis, who became the U.S. secretary of defense in 2017.

Much of a Recon Marine's job includes green operations, which means observing and reporting.

LIVE-ACTION RECON

UNLIKE WORLD WAR II, MOST OPERATIONS DURING THE Vietnam War were relatively small-unit actions. Although these operations often involved fierce fighting, there were few changes of territory. Therefore, they attracted almost no media attention. A notable exception was the Force Recon unit code-named Killer Kane. This group carried out routine intelligence-gathering missions in early 1967. Then a booby trap killed Eric Barnes, a popular officer. It was supposed to be his last mission before heading home. "His death resulted in my changing the tactics employed by my platoon," said team leader First Lieutenant Andrew Finlayson. "I was so incensed by Eric's death that I planned a revenge mission."

During Killer Kane's next mission, Finlayson's team went beyond its assigned patrol sector and set up an ambush along a trail near where Barnes had been killed. Two unsuspecting Viet Cong soldiers came down the trail. They were gunned down and their bodies removed. The same thing happened four hours later. This time, one of the men was an officer with valuable intelligence documents. Finlayson decided that it was too risky to remain there. The unit returned to base camp and celebrated its success.

Killer Kane continued this type of intense action for nine months. Finlayson was especially adept at using air and artillery support as *force multipliers*. He frequently called in artillery on large enemy units. As the enemy retreated, Finlayson

FORCE FACTS The Killer Kane Force Recon platoon of the Vietnam War was named after a villain in the *Buck Rogers* comic strip.

would contact a nearby spotter plane, which added to the carnage with an air strike. Without firing a single shot themselves, the members of Killer Kane often inflicted dozens of casualties.

Not long after Killer Kane's first ambush, the unit was on patrol when the point man heard loud voices. After verifying that no American units were nearby, Finlayson set up another ambush. After several minutes of intense fire from rifles, grenades, and a machine gun, the enemy fled. Finlayson and his men gathered nearly one ton (0.9 t) of equipment. They also retrieved 40 pounds (18.1 kg) of documents, which included codes and equipment lists from a Viet Cong battalion.

Normal combat rotations eventually brought Killer Kane's operations to an end. In all, the unit had conducted more than 30 long-range patrols, killed nearly 500 enemy soldiers, and seized large quantities of documents and supplies. Finlayson received the Bronze Star. The citation read, "With a daring and a flair normally reserved for fictional accounts, Lieutenant Finlayson accumulated a year-long remarkable record." He was a popular subject among prominent U.S. media outlets. He was just as well-known to the enemy, who put a bounty on his head. It was never collected.

Operation Desert Storm is considered one of the most overwhelming American victories in history. In early 1991, U.S. forces inflicted tens of thousands of casualties on Iraqi forces while suffering minimal losses of their own. A five-man Force Recon unit nearly suffered the same fate as those Iraqi soldiers. The team had established a deep reconnaissance observation post on top of a ridgeline 65 miles (105 km) from American lines. They reported that an Iraqi division was positioned a few miles away, between themselves and their fellow Marines.

With little concealment on the ridgeline, the Force Recon position was soon discovered. The team needed a fast ***exfiltration***. But no helicopters were immediately available. An Iraqi battal-

The work of Force Recon in Iraq led to the capture of many Iraqi soldiers.

FORCE FACTS When they halt during missions, Force Recon squads quickly arrange themselves to cover all surrounding viewpoints.

ion numbering more than 250 formed at the base of the ridge. Several F-14 Tomcat fighter aircraft from an offshore aircraft carrier flew low overhead, keeping the battalion at bay. But the planes ran low on fuel and had to depart. Soon afterward, the Iraqis began climbing the ridge. The five Americans readied their weapons. Each man held a grenade with the pin pulled halfway out. By now, the enemy was within 40 yards (35 m) of the unit. Suddenly, a loud clattering announced the arrival of a CH-46 Sea Knight helicopter. With the chopper's heavy machine guns trained on them, the Iraqis halted. As soon as the Sea Knight touched down, the Marines ran to it, scrambled aboard, and flew back to safety.

According to U.S. military authorities, the Second Battle of Fallujah, from November to December 2004, featured some of the heaviest urban combat American forces had faced in nearly 40 years. Force Recon played a key role in the eventual victory. Two days before American, British, and Iraqi government forces launched the assault against *insurgents*, several dozen Force Recon Marines slipped into the city. They sought out insurgent positions and called in artillery strikes just before the battle. This made it easier for the attackers to surge into the city.

In 2004, Abrams tanks provided artillery assistance as Force Recon cleared out insurgents.

It was dangerous work. "We were shooting in all directions," said the leader of one Force Recon platoon. "There were enemy coming out, setting up mortars. There was enemy firing [rocket-propelled grenades], enemy firing machine guns and small arms. We shot all day, at different targets." More than half the platoon suffered casualties, including one Force Recon Marine killed in action. His comrades later killed the insurgent machine gun unit they believed responsible for

his death. Another Marine was more fortunate. He took cover behind a dumpster. Moments later, "[the insurgents] shot an armor-piercing round through that dumpster," he said. "It hit the ground in front of me and bounced off my left forearm. Hit the wall behind me and came back at me." The 1.5-foot-long (0.5 m) projectile, designed to penetrate several inches of steel armor, was a dud. Several weeks of intense fighting followed before the battle ended. "Force Recon provided us with some tremendous capabilities," said one of the American commanders. "I just can't say enough about the job they did."

Force Recon members hone their sniper skills in desert environments to help them in the field.

On September 8, 2010, the *Magellan Star*, a small freighter sailing in the Gulf of Aden off the coast of Yemen, sent a distress signal. Somali pirates were boarding the vessel. The 11 crew members locked themselves in a safe room in the engine compartment. The intruders seized control of the ship. A platoon of Force Recon Marines aboard the USS *Dubuque* had drilled in preparation for such a situation. Now it was time to put their training into action. The men checked and rechecked their equipment and waited for the order that would send them on their way.

Though the *Dubuque* and other warships were close to the *Magellan Star*, the heavily armed pirates acted aggressively, making demands and refusing several calls to surrender. They threatened to shoot anyone who tried to board the ship.

At dawn the next morning, 24 Marines sped toward their target in high-powered inflatable rubber boats. Helicopters hovered nearby, ready to lay down covering fire if needed. Details of the boarding remain classified, but the platoon commander said, "The long and short of it was: some of the enemy threw their hands up when rifles were put in their face, some ran and attempted to elude us in the superstructure but were run down, and some hesitated but were taken down by less than *lethal* force, as the situation dictated. The end result was 9 pirates captured in an opposed boarding and 11 crew members rescued." Not a single shot was fired.

Countless other stories attest to the value of Force Recon. Today, however, a certain amount of tension is still present between MARSOC and Force Recon. Major General Frederick Padilla says, "A lot of reconnaissance Marines are exactly what MARSOC is looking for, but we still have a requirement for reconnaissance Marines. So we have to make more of them, and it's not easy to make reconnaissance Marines. You don't do it overnight." The delicate balancing act between the need for both forces is likely to continue. One thing is certain: recon is a vital element for success in battle. There will always be a place for Marines skilled in searching out information about the enemy.

★★★

A Force Recon platoon resolved the hostage situation aboard the Magellan Star *without using lethal force.*

FORCE FACTS Force Recon has a (mostly) friendly rivalry with Navy SEALs because both groups specialize in maritime operations.

A large part of training for Force Recon is aquatic competency and physical endurance.

FORCE FACTS Camp Lejeune is named for Lieutenant General John Lejeune, Marine Corps commandant from 1920 to 1929 who was called the "greatest of all leathernecks." (Leatherneck is another name for a Marine.)

GLOSSARY

U.S. SPECIAL FORCES

amphibious – involving forces landed from the sea

atolls – coral reefs including small islands encircling a lagoon

breaching – breaking through a barrier

casualties – people injured or killed in an accident or a battle

embedded – attached to a military unit

enlisted – describing those who sign up voluntarily or are drafted for military duty at a rank below an officer; they compose the largest part of military units

exfiltration – removal of personnel from enemy-controlled territory

extractions – safe withdrawals from a mission

feint – a distracting movement meant to mislead an enemy

fragmentation – when describing grenades, a type that emits sharp metal particles upon detonation

force multipliers – capabilities that significantly increase the firepower of a combat force

foregrip – the handle of a weapon mounted under the front part of the barrel

Global Positioning System – a navigation system using 24 orbiting satellites located more than 10,000 miles above Earth

improvised – produced without advance preparation from available materials

incendiary – intended to start fires

infrastructure – physical and organizational structures essential for the operation of a society

insertions – secretly putting troops into an area likely to be controlled by an enemy

insurgents – rebels; those in armed resistance to a government

intelligence – information about movements and strength of forces of an enemy

lethal – likely to cause death

mole – a spy who achieves an important position within a country's defense systems over a long period of time and uses that position to pass along sensitive information

parafoil – a fabric device similar to a parachute and shaped like an airplane wing

recoilless – describing lightweight artillery that counteracts and reduces the normal recoil movement of rifles

rucksacks – backpacks made of strong, waterproof material and often associated with the military

squad automatic weapon – a lightweight machine gun offering a portable source of automatic weaponry to a small unit

SELECTED BIBLIOGRAPHY

U.S. SPECIAL FORCES

Bohrer, David. *America's Special Forces*. St. Paul, Minn.: MBI, 2002.

Clancy, Tom, with Gen. Carl Stiner and Tony Koltz. *Shadow Warriors: Inside the Special Forces*. New York: Putnam's, 2002.

Eward, J. Kenneth. *US Marine Corps Recon and Special Operations Uniforms & Equipment 2000–15*. Oxford: Osprey, 2016.

Frederick, Jim. *Special Ops: The Hidden World of America's Toughest Warriors*. New York: Time Books, 2011.

Lanning, Michael Lee, and Ray William Stubbe. *Inside Force Recon: Recon Marines in Vietnam*. New York: Ballantine Books, 1989.

Melson, Charles D., Paul Hannon, and Lee Johnson. *Marine Recon, 1940–90*. London: Osprey, 1994.

Pushies, Fred J. *Marine Force Recon*. St. Paul, Minn.: MBI, 2003.

Tucker, David, and Christopher J. Lamb. *United States Special Operations Forces*. New York: Columbia University Press, 2007.

WEBSITES

Five Kids Activities to Do Reconnaissance

http://www.freakyrivet.com/blog/activity-posts/5-kids-activities-to-do-reconnaissance/

Read about activities kids can do to learn some basic techniques involved in successful reconnaissance missions.

US Marines Force Recon Training – USMC Force Recon Training

https://www.youtube.com/watch?v=gshBDiDBHnk

This documentary shows the training and simulated battlefield experiences of Force Recon, including interviews with personnel.

READ MORE

Brush, Jim. *Special Forces*. Mankato, Minn.: Sea-to-Sea, 2012.

Cooper, Jason. *U.S. Special Operations*. Vero Beach, Fla.: Rourke, 2004.

Note: Every effort has been made to ensure that the websites listed above have educational value and that they contain no inappropriate material. However, because of the nature of the Internet, it is impossible to guarantee that these sites will remain active indefinitely or that their contents will not be altered.

INDEX

U.S. SPECIAL FORCES